REBEL WITHOUT APPLAUSE

For Pat,
The Best Wish
Great School
Thanks

[signature]

92.

REBEL WITHOUT APPLAUSE

LEMN SISSAY

BLOODAXE BOOKS

Copyright © Lemn Sissay 1992

ISBN: 1 85224 202 7

First published 1992 by
Bloodaxe Books Ltd,
P.O. Box 1SN,
Newcastle upon Tyne NE99 1SN.

Bloodaxe Books Ltd acknowledges
the financial assistance of Northern Arts.

Cover printing by J. Thomson Colour Printers Ltd, Glasgow.

Printed in Great Britain by
Cromwell Press Ltd, Broughton Gifford, Melksham, Wiltshire.

for Kadifa Williams

Acknowledgements

Poems from this book have been broadcast on *Celebration* (Granada Television), *Packet of Three* (Channel Four), and *Clarke Productions* (TVS); on the BBC Radio 4 programmes *Kaleidoscope*, *Poetry Now*, and *Young Playwrights Festival*; on BBC Radio 5's *Fanshawe on Five*, *The Mix*, and *Up North*; and on various regional BBC radio stations including Bristol, Leeds, Sheffield and Manchester.

Acknowledgements are due to the editors of the following publications in which some of these poems first appeared: *Artrage*, *The Bees Knees* (Stride Publications, 1990), *City Limits*, *The Face*, *The New British Poetry* (Paladin, 1988), *Poetry Review*, *Slice of the Sky* (Heinemann, 1992), *The Sun Rises in the North* (Smith/Doorstop Books, 1992), *Sunk Island Review*, and *Tender Fingers in a Clenched Fist* (Bogle-L'Ouverture, 1988)

Many thanks to Jessica Huntley and Eric Huntley.

Contents

If you are a big tree
I am the small axe

BOB MARLEY

Bearing Witness

dedicated to James Baldwin who in his last recorded interview said black writers should bear witness to the times.

Bearing witness to the times
where it pays to sell lines
where African thighs thrive for twenty-five
and guns run with the midnight son.

Bearing witness to the days
of the blue-eyed glaze
in the black-eyed girl of the world
whose life depends on a contact lens.

Bearing witness to the screams
of children cut on shattered dreams,
colonialised minds lost in times
of permanent frowns and nervous breakdowns.

Bearing witness to the signs
of white sandstorms in black minds,
of waves from the west with white dagger crests
scratching the black beaches back.

Bearing witness to the hour
where maladjusted power
realigns its crimes in token signs
then perversely repents with self-punishment.

Bearing witness to the times
where black people define
the debt yet to be paid, you bet
I'll be rhyming the fact when I witness that.

Remember How We Forgot

We don't cram around the radio any more.
We have arrived at the multi-dimensional war
where diplomats chew it up and spew it up
and we stand like orphans with empty cups.
'There will be no peace' the press release
said the likelihood of war is on the increase.
We are being soaked in a potion,
massaged with a lotion to calm the commotion
that hides the embers of the fire.
There's nothing as quick as a liar.
Don't you learn your lesson?
Are you so effervescent that
when they say day is day and it's dark in your window
you say OK and listen more tomorrow?
Seems you heard the trigger word.
You are space to be replaced, your dreams defaced.
Heavy questions quickly sink
leaving no trace – a spiked drink.
What kind of trip are you on?
Don't you remember the last one?
Remember how we forgot about Vietnam,
Afghanistan, will you fall or stand
for a dream you haven't seen?
I'm afraid you will, you've taken the pill.
You're totally stoned on war.

Media hype and the slogans they write,
is that all it takes to set you alight?
There's nothing better than a doped mind
for a young unemployed man to sign.
Figures go down when young men sign up.
What better when they're losing the votes, than to erupt
into the uniting sound of war fever.
'We need unity now more than ever...
We shall only attack to righteously defend!'
Paranoia seeps in:
'Are you one of us or one of them?'

Slogans fall like hard rain as the government calls
for its children to break down the walls,
of someone somewhere in some country
that is suddenly so vital to history.
Young men hang in their own fear...
But we don't cover that story, not here,
not when we are in a battle that must be won.
Don't you understand there's a war going on.
More than ever we should pull together
these are days of stormy weather
where the patriots show their faces
and nationalists recruit places.
As the fear of the foreigner arises,
the race attack count rises,
victims of the small island mentality.
England is no Mother country.
He holds the fear of The Awakening,
of his shivering shores breaking
like those in the Middle East did
when he raped it.
Will you take it, take this, without question
fall in line with the press and the politician?
Remember how we forgot about Vietnam,
Afghanistan, will you fall or stand
for a dream you haven't seen?
I'm afraid you will, you've taken the pill.
You're totally stoned on war.

Wake Up Niggers II

(rap: with thanks to Jalal Nurridin, who wrote 'Wake Up Niggers')

Dreams can become an hallucinogenic form
close the window forget the storm,
notch a hole and crawl inside
with flimsy clichés to prop the pride.
But you can't hide from your own.
You must come out, the wind has blown
and when the light burns in the heat of these days
it will cut like a cutlass that clutch of clichés.
Wake up niggers before we're all dead.
One day you'll suck those teeth into the back of your head.
Wake up niggers before we are all dead.
The first step of the journey is the longest we tread.

In a misty morning when the sky pulls up the sun
you may awake to the click of the barrel of the gun,
or hear the solid banging from your own front door.
Through the letterbox you reply you don't do the pools any more.
The storm in a teacup can shatter your being
in juxtaposed shock you shall lose all your meaning,
saying things like 'How can it be so,
how can I tape Millie Jackson if they've smashed my video.'

It isn't reactionary it is quickly becoming fact
we need to pull together for political combat
to sink into the bill, see the mood of the clause.
Why the strange letter to my African father
         about the immigration laws.
Like the nightmare this country is closing in
Europe for the Europeans, the new slogan of skin
and we were too busy listening to some sweet tune
too busy throwing our words to the moon.
Too busy to realise the pen had begun to stifle
for it was no longer a pen but a green jacket and rifle
and before we know it Moss Side is akin to Northern Ireland,
and the neighbourly face, cold and hardened.
And you pinch yourself – is this a dream,
Is all really what it seems?

Wake up niggers before we are all dead
The first step of the journey is the longest we tread.

Fingerprints

I can see your fingerprints
fumbled all over this dead boy's body,
can see them in his
lifeless eyes,
in his fist clutched
by rigor mortis,
and holding up your hands to calm us people
you say: 'This was not a racial attack.'

I can see the wipe marks
on his forehead
where with the side of your fist
you tried to wipe them in

      smudge them in
         reshape them
            rub them in
        distort them
          change them
            hide them
      rearrange them

    With ink that dried
        before he died

You report:
'We understand the victim was Black
this was not a racial attack.'

Gold from the Stone

Water cupped in hands
Taken from the stream
Brought upon a laughing land
Through the mouth of a scream

Gold from the stone
Oil from the earth
I yearned for my home
From the time of my birth

Strength of a mother's whisper
Shall carry me until
The hand of my lost sister
Joins onto my will

Root to the earth
Blood from the heart
Could never from birth
Be broken apart

Food from the platter
Water from the rain
The subject and the matter
I'm going home again

Can't sell a leaf to a tree
Nor the wind to the atmosphere
I know where I'm meant to be
And I can't be satisfied here

Can't give light to the moon
Nor mist to the drifting cloud
I shall be leaving here soon
Costumed cultured and crowned

Can't give light to the sun
Nor a drink to the sea
The earth I must stand on
I shall kiss with my history

Sugar from the cane
Coal from the wood
Water from the rain
Life from the blood

Gold from the stone
Oil from the earth
I yearned for my home
Ever since my birth

Food from the platter
Water from the rain
The subject and the matter
I'm going home again

Occupations

I don't need an occupation
to get picked up on the street.
I don't need an occupation
to be the victim of deceit.

I don't need an occupation
to get my pockets searched.
I don't need an occupation
to get kicked where it hurts.

I don't need an occupation
for basic rights to be taken away.
I don't need an occupation
to visit the cells for a day.

I don't need an occupation
to be living underneath.
I don't need an occupation
to feel a boot within my teeth.

I don't need an occupation
to be pestered constantly.
I don't need an occupation
to be hounded by the beast.

They are getting paid
when they're harassing me,
when they're writing out
false confessions of a robbery

and in the cells I felt a rhyme
riddle with a rhythm inside of me,
if the judgement fits the crime
get them when they're off duty.

Boiling Up

Can you spread me lightly on this street?
I would like to blend in.
If butter and bread can do it, so can I.

Will you sprinkle me softly in this hotel?
I would like to blend in.
If chicken and seasoning can do it, so can I.

(The store detective is either trying to
strike up some kind of meaningful relationship with me
or I've got a box of jelly babies stuck to my left ear.)

Could you drip me into this club?
I would like to blend in.
If coffee and milk can do it, so can I.

(It's not a sawn-off shot-gun in my inside pocket,
and that's not because I keep my machete there –
ten Regal King Size please.)

Can you grate me into this city?
I would like to blend in.
If cheese and tomatoes can do it, so can I.

Can you soak me into this country?
I would like to blend in.
If rice and peas can do it, so can I.

Images of Africa

Africa, land of milk and honey.
That is, riches sucked from the African oasis
thin stock and economical crises
the democratic dilemma of medicinal shortage
the historically legalised theft of a language,
dollars spiked in bayonet-crowned guns
puncturing the horizon, silhouetting the sun.

Africa, land of light and sunshine
that cuts like a razor on dry tired lips
reminiscent of blood-licking whips
which can still be heard in the land owned
in the echo of the African moan.
A land spat on by the Victorian age
that locked its water in a living stone cage.

Africa bright and bustling streets.
Blood running from trickle to stream,
dripping from the thirsty lips of the American dream,
pulped with the hammer struck with the sickle,
cheated of riches, a cheat returns little
but for riddles to belittle unification.
Not a first not a second but a third world malformation.

Africa a paradise untouched and new-found
clasped by its neck in the iron fist,
fractured and isolated by the anthropologist,
locked in the colonised minds of slaves
which talk of better lives across bloody waves.
Haunted and taunted by the twisted historian,
the net has yet to catch your spirit, African.

Instant Consciousness

Instant consciousness comes in the pound,
pay at the town hall and spread it around.
Love it or hate it who are we to debate it
we're so glad you've got it and daren't underrate it

because now you can serve us with the new vision
teach all us blacks about multiculturalism,
then propose that if we don't listen to you
we're as bad as the rest, we're racist too.

It comes in a packet doesn't cause no pain
you buy it in toilets no guilt and no shame.
The councillor says it's the product of the day
there's money in it and you don't have to pay.

It's taken us so long, you get there so fast,
getting jobs to stop harassment while we get harassed.
Thanks for inviting me to dinner, I think I'm getting fat.
Instant Consciousness, I'd love some more of that.

Airmail to a Dictionary

Black is...the shawl of the night
secure from sharp paranoic light

Black is...the pupil of the eye
putting colour in the sea's skin and earthen sky

Black is...the oil of the engine
on which this whole world is depending

Black is...light years of space
holding on its little finger this human race

Black is...the colour of ink
that makes the history books we print

Black is...the army. Wars in the night
putting on the Black to hide the white

Black is...the colour of coal
giving work to the miners, warmth to the old

Black is...the shade of the tree
sharp in definition against inequality

Black is...the eclipse of the sun
displaying its power to every one

Black is...the ink from a history
that shall redefine the dictionary

Black on Black is Black is Black is
strong as asphalt and tarmac is

Black is...a word that I love to see
Black is that, yeah, black is me

The Customs Men

Breaking out from the plane
home's mouth lays wide open
from the white oesophagus corridors
guarded by the English custom of suspicion,
and to prove my situation
I have written this so that

when they have fingered their
dirty hands through my clothes,
mauled my enjoyable flight
with personal questions,
pricked a little for reaction
and arrived at my book

I will point them to this poem
simply to tell them
that I get job satisfaction, in the end,
and they will get nothing but tobacco beneath their nails.

Mind-walking

1

A stray sunshot caught
his heart.

As a child
he spent time
melting
   dripping
like a fallen lolly on a kerb
in summer.

As a child
he teased questions from his
black-topped brain,
like he'd
lick the bowl when his mother left
the kitchen.

There was always one ultimate question
that arose
while building
mud pies
or staring at cobwebs in hedges.

Only as the full line itched his tongue,
as it had unravelled from his thoughts like a red carpet,
only when the gravity of his question became its heaviest,
unbearable almost
would he race home and
stand with the urgency
of a young boy desperate for a pee.
'Mum mum',

who was doing the same thing as he
but in the kitchen,

'If the earth is
            spinning why doesn't it move
        if I jump up and
why aren't I dizzy...?

A stray sun shot caught
her heart
she would call it
brain-strolling or mind-walking
said he'd walk into church
one day and say
'why is God not here'.
On studiously receiving a stiff reply
he'd look at the cross and say
'well he doesn't have to hang about like that
he can have my seat'.

2

A stray sun-shot bled into
his heart

    welled in his chest
    crept up the inside of his eyelids,

curdled through his whip-like lashes
down the bright brown bony cheeks.

    He had run till his breath
    was almost too far ahead of him.

He had run till his heartbeat
had overtaken his pounding feet,

    till the rustle of the trees
    had taken his breath,

till the squawk of a magpie
had overtaken the rustle of the trees,

    till the rattle of the keys
    had overtaken the squawk of a magpie.

He had run till his breath
was almost too far ahead of him,

It filled the kitchen and his mother
listened to it counting
400 years
of panting.
She heard her
grandfather in him,
her grandmother's wheeze
her father's defiance
her husband's private sobbing
at being broken,
She listened until
the room was filled with spirits
ricocheting from wall to wall,
cradled in the sink
dripping from the ceiling.
Clinging to their necks like weak motherless children...

Here was a question he would ask them
and it would twist their bodies each time.

For My Headstone

Here is the death of the son you never had
the hand you never touched
the face you never stroked

here is the morning after
his bruises you never tended
the laughter you never shared

and here are the tears he'll never feel
your eyes he'll never see
whispers he'll never hear
the apologies
will squirm in his coffin
with the letters you never wrote.

Love Poem

You remind me
define me
incline me.

If you died
I'd.

Flowers in the Kitchen

On buying her flowers
she said

'There's no food in the kitchen
and we can't eat flowers.'

On buying her food
she said

'You don't buy flowers any more.'

Suitcases and Muddy Parks

You say I am a lying child
I say I'm not
you say there you go again

You say I am a rebellious child
I say no I'm not
you say there you go again

Quite frankly mum
I've never seen a rebellious child before
and when my mates said
jump in that puddle and race you through the park
(y'know the muddy one)
I didn't think about the mud.

When you said why are you dirty!
I could feel the anger in your voice
I still don't know why.

I said I raced my mates through the park.
You said it was deliberate.
I said I didn't I mean I did but it wasn't.
You said I was lying,
I said no I am not.
You said there you go again.

Later in the dawn of adolesence
it was time for my leave
I with my suitcased social worker,
you with your husband,
walked our sliced ways.

Sometimes I run back to you
like a child through a muddy park,
adult achievements tucked under my arm,
I explain them with a child-like twinkle,
thinking any mother would be proud...

Your eyes, desperately trying to be wise and unrevealing,
    reveal all.
Still you fell back into the heart of the same rocking chair
    saying there you go again.

And I did.
And I have.

The Nest

In shells
small bells
echo
echoes

till the hairline crack
hisses

revealing
small chickens.

That's us:

small chickens
learning to hatch.

Different eggs
in the same nest.

Autumn

Used to wake up in your smile
and kiss the corner of your lips
but autumn eyes
on winter mornings
close
like the curtains of my new flat.

Like those crisp leaves
we've curled up,
are brittle,
crackle and crumble at a touch.
It's a sad beauty in autumn,
a scruffy tatty end,
dulled and numbed.

Pass It On
(rap)

How is it that we still smile when the pressure comes?
How is it that we stand firm when they think that we should run?
How is it that we retain our integrity?
How is it through this maze that we keep the clarity?
How is it that through pain we retain compassion?
How is it that we spread but stay one nation?
How is it that we work in the face of abuse?
How is it that the pressure's on yet we seem loose?
This is the story about the rising truth,
when you feel closed in simply raise the roof,
the Africans were the first civilisation
born by the Nile was the first generation.

Malcolm X had a dream we have a dream too,
and the only way to get it is to pass it on through,
from the day we leave to the day we arrived
we were born to survive born to stay alive,
by all means necessary I'm an accessory,
to provide the positive vibe is a necessity,
to clasp our past to go to war with our fears
to claim and attain in our future years.
Sometimes life can be cold and complicated
more time the problem is overrated.
Nina Simone called it the Backlash Blues
even though they say it's history we all know that it's news.

The oppressor hopes and prays for you to cry
to close your hearts and your minds to lay down and die,
to be another numb number to treat and delete
to fall into the spiral rhythm of defeat.
Malcolm X had a dream we have a dream too
and the only way to get it is to pass it on through
no message has been stronger, no sea carried more weight,
no army marched for longer, no wind swept at this rate,
so pride in my skin is in the vision I have seen.
The pain I withstand for I have a dream.
Know who you are, know the ground on which you stand.
Never build your house on a bed of sand.

Island Mentality

It's no wonder
the Brits enjoy the scenery.
It's no wonder
that they play games like Scrabble and Monopoly.
It's no wonder
that they get engrossed in Trivial Pursuits.
It's no wonder
that they work for Saturday night to puke.
It's no wonder
that they're frightened, the plain reality
is that this dot on my world map is hemmed in by the sea.

It's no wonder
that Brits get sick of where they live.
It's no wonder
that every other culture's treated like a myth.
It's no wonder
that so many are twisted with hate.
It's no wonder
that they generalise instead of trying to relate.
The truth is clear it's obvious to me
this dot on my world map is hemmed in by the sea.

It's no wonder
that the clubs are so claustrophobic.
It's no wonder
that these people get a buzz out of being sick.
It's no wonder
that they say we take their jobs and their woman.
It's no wonder
that they feel they are missing something.
Their broken pride is based on fantasy.
This ink blot on my world map is hemmed in by the sea.
Hemmed in by the sea, hemmed in by the sea
I can walk on water and you cannot chase me.

Going Places

Another
cigarette ash
television serial filled
advert analysing
cupboard starving
front room filling
tea slurping
mind chewing
brain burping
carpet picking
pots watching
room gleaning
toilet flushing
night,
with nothing to do

I think I'll paint roads
on my front room walls
to convince myself
that I'm going places.

Gil Scott Heron

Gil Scott Heron shines
in tightly cut rhythmic rhymes.

The Harlem hero strikes again,
jazz in the house, milk the pain.

From politics in poetics
the symbols in the lyrics

shut in the drum ripple in the skin
while the bass dives deep and digs in.

Gil Scott Heron shines
in tightly cut rhythmic rhymes

the Washington wonder strikes again
jazz in the house, milk the pain.

And Brian Jackson in zoot suite
places into the root the sweet flute,

black and in Britain we know what Scott means
when he documents the siege of New Orleans,

with subtlety in vibes and lyrics giving clues
the man talks in colours in the inner city blues,

explained how television would not be revolutionised
and how the revolution would not be televised.

This panther is black catch its silhouette
cutting a shadow to outline the debt.

Martin Luther King and a cut of Malcolm X
wrapped in the musical strength of the Amnesia Express.

Gil Scott Heron shines
in tightly cut rhythmic lines

Another black hero strikes again
jazz in the house, milk the pain.

Godsell

You knock upon my door
and open
I drink to you.
This is a bad trip,
something about Armageddon
and pigs possessed by devils
flinging themselves from cliffs.
Look back into my house and I may turn to salt.

Blackened horizons itch with locusts,
whole pieces of earth slump
swallowed by the devil's breath;
Yea as I walk through the valley of death
with Lucifer in the crick of my back
an avalanche of commands befalls me
and I whimper from the cross and catapult
in the child's hand,
clutching a lock of my own hair,
feeling the heat of a burning bush
singe the back of my neck.
Three score and ten years of this;
look back into my house and I may turn to salt.

Where is the chariot of fire
where is the chariot of fire.
I, one piece of thirty pieces of silver ,
a possessed pig, laugh at the cliff's edge,
snort and fling myself to the rocks.

When I meet Peter
I shall bribe him,
as I have been bribed.

Euroman

Darwin's theory has proven right
Euro man has seen the light.
He speaks in English speaks in French
watches dramas with Judi Dench.

Spends his time playing draughts
drinks cheap wine. He's fuckin daft.
Plays tennis, eats courgettes.
Does he play bingo? Does he eck.

Euroman is a children's chap,
good to get on with and full of crap.
Smug as an Aran jumper the wrong way on
he doesn't say good. He says *bon*.

He's got shares in Perrier
and speaks out of his derrière.
He only buys his fish in Cannes
Does he go to Blackpool? Not Euroman.

Flushed

Why
Can't
Heads
Have
Overflow pipes
    Like toilets
    If
    They
    Did
    I
    Could
    Pull
    My
    Ear
    And
    Flush
    It
    All
    Out.

I Hate You

You're as popular as a posted
birthday gift to someone who's just died.
I once said you weren't that bad,
I lied.

You're a conversation number,
your presence binds lips together.
Why is it when your name is mentioned
there's a sudden change of weather?

You're a lift to a claustrophobic
a witch to a priest.
You're gushy and gooey.
You're my release.

I wouldn't be a bell ringer
with a face like that.
Here see how hard you can
head butt this cricket bat.

How can we discuss the meaning of life
when you don't deserve it.
It's a bad habit that, breathing,
I wish you could curb it.

It's short and sweet
and there isn't much pain,
have you ever tried hang-gliding
without a plane.

I'd say I didn't mean all this
but truthfully I'd be lying
and I really wouldn't write it
if I thought that you'd be crying.

In fact if I was you I wouldn't
see any need for resentment
because from me to you, quite honestly,
this has got to be a compliment.

A Black Man on the Isle of Wight

Faces cold as the stones stuck
to the sea's belly
with seaweed for hair
sculpted into expressions of fear.

Professional Black

Whirlwinds attract you more than the common breeze.
It's too easy to see the wood and never the trees.
You can make a tailor-made struggle just for the stage
and the government will fund it cos it's all the rage.

And you can fool the bodies into giving you the readies
because only black people can define just where your head is,
when I check it out the hammer hits upon the nail
you speak about the struggle as if it was a fairy tale.

As if it was a vehicle, your personal limousine
with closed and tainted windows to take you to your dream
and the only ones who see this are the ones who realise
that you're cheating this 'community' with lies.

You disagree with these words and theatrically deny
telling me what you've done for black people, never telling me why
and there before my eyes it became totally apparent
that you were never black, simply transparent.

Pretoria Pit

I lived next to Pretoria,
a deformed tongue of earth
holding fathers and sons in clenched stone throats.

Young estate kids stole motorbikes
wheel spinning on the fossilised spines of miners
who groaned in the trips of hippies
who plucked magic mushrooms from their mouths.

In parts, on sharp sides, silver birches scream for light
like the flame breathing canaries.
Pretoria bleeds in still pond pockets.

And I'd sit on this and watch the sun through
the dead mill windows; make it look
like a church, like it was crying
like the whole Lancashire plain was mourning
as the souls rose through the birch trees
and suckled the stars.

Our estate hunched at Pretoria's feet
fell down from there,
as if in awe
as if running away down into the village
desperate to break through onto Market Street.

Mill Town and Africa

How many fingernails of my own shall I pluck
till she sees that my blood is hers.
Revolutions have passed between us,
emperors dethroned, guns and red flags raised.
Churches have crumbled, stampeding our pathways.
Governments have collapsed.
We scattered on different sides of the debris.

While I wiped sweat and coaldust from my face,
wiping sweat and sanddust from her face
I saw her over the Lancashire Plain
fleeing Ethiopia with the remnants of a family.
She had washed into the hard Manchester rain
and I into the skating heatwave.

She became more to me than this
I would dream her, awake with a picture
see her on a London bus, unblinking.

Uncle Tom and the 1990s

The way he
bowed his head to the lilac princess,
and spat on the young black boy

polished his shoes and ignored the news
of the lynching in his own backyard

or folded his clothes and held up his nose
at the sounds of a screaming sister:

Uncle Tom, the same syllable sound
as true or false, sweet and sour,
right or wrong do or die,

is dead
manacled mutilated moaning in his grave
twisting and turning in all the suppressed unrest.

He sweeps the floors of hell.
Licks the walls of heaven,
takes all the sinners to the pit of eternal fire,
children, crinkly old men, crimson young girls;
holds them by the hand, tells them
they'll be all right, they'll get used to it, and hums

'Oh lordy pick a bale of souls
Oh Lordy pick a bale a day
Gonna jump down turn around pick a bale of souls
everydoghasitsdayhewholivestorunawayifatfirstyoudon't
succeedabirdinthehandisbettereyesbiggerthanyouranger
begatsangerdon'trocktheboat'

Frustrated black people still pull him from the grave
but the myth
has decomposed and doesn't hold together
the years between then and now.

We are at the crux of making
a martyr from a fool
a fool from a martyr

Uncle Tom is dead
Hot oil spittle pours from each orifice
his solidified words...
'Everycloudhasathere'sgoodandbadinweareallthesameunder
liveandletlive'

Make him a saint or a swear word
both are a modern day charade.

There is no uncle tom in the 1990s,
just cold calculated black moving sculpture, sharp and sinister,
who know exactly what they're doing.

Clear as Day Storms

It's in the secluded moment
or the hectic deadlines
that beyond my control
I remember the times
when skies bent with red strength,
to protect our innocent minds,
would paint pathways home
for memories to find.

But moon soaked storms
(as we swam against the tide
or circled like eagles
above the mountain sides),
dragged me
into the hurricane's eye
and sucked me through
darkened skies;

through ricocheted demands
commands too high to reach,
grey rooms, rattling keys,
and corridors too bleached.
With no space to breathe
I would sit by the window pane
to watch the storm stabbing
and the night time cry in pain.

And now in the night's whisper
and the single magpie's lull,
as the air thick and humid
and the wind begins to pull,
I greet the storm,
stand in its rain
and somehow you're as clear
as the day again.

Another Brother's Sister

All pissed up and nowhere to go,
she could've gone somewhere but who's to know
as she slips into the streets
pushes out the pleats
and never awakens tomorrow.

Who's to guess
who's next
which friend bends
as the pressure lends
itself to a crick in the neck.

There'll be the usual funeral crowd
quiet in the frown
of a hot summer's day
sparkling with arrays
of flowers cryin out loud.

A relative from times
of whispered nursery rhymes
may slowly emerge
on the glass-slippery verge
and remember her giggles at lines.

Introduction in Transit

And tears were sleeping
with no earthly reason
to wet her breasts.

Oblivious in adventure
she peered into the heavens;
hollow tunnels, riddled with pirates.

Britain, shaped like a begging dog
beckoned the steel eagle to land.
'Home soon,' the engines whispered

meanwhile, furrowed with wrinkles
her father who wished her so well
let go of his smile.

She, introduced
like a lamb to the butcher
with grass in his hand.

My Brother

We laughed, played draughts
under a sweeping sleeping sun
by the coconut tree
and the smell of lemon grass.
He had returned from Paris.

It took us half an hour
to get the right coconut
and two minutes to mix the juice
with raspberry cordial.
That night I cried
how alike we could have been.

Gunshot

(rap)

Another brother falls
another mother calls
another family wants to break down the walls
and cry for their son that died.
Some live and try to live a lie.
Cold mornings and preachers bow heads
in respect for a dead youth.
The truth crouches behind the hearse
between the lines of a poet's verse.
Someone lost a son or a daughter caught
by the peacock chest of an angry man with red eye.
Live by the sword and die.
Politicians condemn them, police swell
and follow the funeral parade, too afraid
to walk they send helicopters and SWAT teams.
These are not South Africa's but Moss Side's screams.
Those who know those who live hide,
one man dies to another tide of revenge
and so the chain reacts with no end.

Everyone knows someone who's died
cos everyone knows everyone,
it's village mentality with grenades,
who's afraid of the big bad wolf
I'm not 'cept for when he's carrying a gun.
The air is calm but the people in it frenetic
paranoic, nervous and itching for a fight,
setting the world alight or at least my area.
An endless tide of processions
dark against the grey skies.
A black shroud throngs the street,
someone has died.
The press's hound-dogs pelting through the estates
mugging stories and selling them like coke.

They steam in with crow bars,
opening up lives better closed,
scaffolding black mouths
crawling into the coffin
to get an interview with the dead man.
The police bust the wrong homes
as the preacher throws the soil,
bring in the wrong folks,
as a sister lays a wreath.
It's a chicken run over here.
As a group of children cross the road to church
helicopter blades slice the air above.
Police wagons curl on the corner
and heads turn to them.

Children and Company

It's children who spot sand-pits
and large puddles
insect spit
and warm cuddles.

It's children who spot spiders
and dew-cobbled cobwebs
holes in bushes
and worms that are half dead.

It's children who spot puddles
pavement cracks and kerbs
cement between bricks
and brand new verbs.

It's children who spot grandad
picking at his nose
the stubble on his chin
the smell on his clothes.

It's children who spot shadows
disguised as monsters
and brown knotty sticks
to chuck at the conkers.

It's children who spot scruffy dogs
and skinny cats
and bird nests in the tweed
of an old flat cap.

It's children who spot broken-legged blackbirds
and the biggest caterpillar
the one with the fangs
that had to be a killer.

Negotiations

For the radical faction to change the constitution
They should take their allegations to the institution
So we took our allegations with a big bag of patience
Before we even met we felt the pain of prejudgement
But we'd set up the meeting, gave the standard greeting
And if vibes could harm us we'd have got a good beating
But the minutes were restricted and the picture they depicted
Was nothing but a smutter of the things we had presented

But onward we went with constructive intention
Keeping our strengths from personal friction
But keeping the prevention of personal pretention
Was keeping construction in total detention
Resulting in destruction and bad vibrations

And a cut in the bag that was holding the patience.
And a cut in the bag that was holding the patience.
And a cut in the bag that was holding the patience.

Writers Blockocks

Instead of rolling my tongue around a juicy adjective
while finding myself an abstract objective
to metaphorically master through a perfect perspective
and economically edit to its utmost connective,
I find myself lost in a cell full of words
I know what I want to do but I can't find the verbs.
Rhymes are on the run through the keyhole and under the door
saying I am going to die a death if you use me any more.

But a padded cell is not enough it's another cliché
another padded out and poached piece of poetry today.
My illness is spreading pathetic as the odd sock
and the fact that that gets me to the rhyme that I've got
      writer's block.
Grief wells, haunting my paper with cunning and clarity
to see this block, the big full stop, the end to my literacy.
Suicide seems to be the only recurring choice
for on top of all this, I'm an oral poet and I think I'm losing
      my voice!

Europe the Resurgence
(rap)

Take a look into your history books
Remember how you was taught, how Columbus fought.
Familiarise yourself with European thought.
Conquer was the word I heard that replaced genocide,
voyage across the sea the real death ride.
White people came to claim and rename
where there was peace they introduced pain.
In the name of economics and the Holy Trinity
the Europeans introduced slavery to our world.
The British the Spanish the French and the Danes
all went to Africa to make their claim,
gunpowder power understand the mentality
it's documented well, they called it history.
Ladened with wealth in the bellies of their ships
they travelled on a sea of gunpowder and whips.
It is evil in the rawest sense
to kill another man with no defence.

I resent what I am finding and that it's taken as read
that the past is past and past is dead.
But the frozen soil of its grave is breaking
the European tribe is once again awakening
I'm looking for solace for some kind of good
but all that I am finding is pools of black blood
in the hands of Europeans, in the mouths of the Boers,
in the African townships, on the Gambian shores.
It makes me sick; blood like an oil slick
on which they travelled back home, heroes anointed by the queen
tall stories of the places they'd been
of savages cannibals, look at your TV
then you will see how this relates to me.
They were looking for something that we had inside
a oneness of being a solid self-pride.
Maybe I should miss this but being an analyst,
all is related to what is generated
I feel it must be stated, that underneath this stone
there is a beast and it is beginning to groan.

The Black Moon

Some would say there was no moon
if it was black, becauses it can't be seen
with the naked eye,
like there is a naked eye
unattached to a brain.

I would say take a closer look,
here use this telescope
point it towards that star.
Yes the white and bright one
can you relate to that, right,
now move it to the left...up a little

An outline, a circular shape
that's the one, yeah! Yes that's the black moon.
A circular magnificence reveals and breathes
itself into another mind, free again.
The music of knowing.

Taking his eye away
quizzically, mockingly he said
Yeah but what do I want to know that for.

All that investigation
all that proof

For what?

Think I'll use my energy showing
a black man a black moon.

Because this hurts too much.

Can You Locate Planet Ethnic?

Peace. There is one world; we've learned something. Peace. There are vast and different cultures within it. Peace. Each wants happiness. Peace. Each has differing criteria to attain happiness. Peace. Wanting to reach the same place does not mean to say that we are the same race or the same face. Peace. I am not an ethnic, there is no Ethnicia. I can't locate planet Ethnic, could you direct me to the Nicaraguan samosas please? Peace. We are all individuals I'm told. Strange cos I thought I was a portion of sweet and sour chicken. When a mathematician explains sums there is no need to inform him that he is using numbers. Peace.

There is a movement. I've been moved. I used to be black and now I'm a samosa-eating ethnic. Peace. Cynicism and guilt are the death of people's movement. Peace. So move quick and keep moving quick. Peace. I crawled from the melting pot a long time ago, because the largest ingredient had an overpowering flavour. Peace. I crawled from the melting pot. Peace. Here is the salad bowl where there are distinctly different ingredients, together, forming a wholesome enrichness. Peace. Is the anti-racism movement anti-race? Peace. I am a Black man. Peace. Another interviewer asserts that I'm a man. She is so right (I glimpse the badge and keep an open mind), I am a man, a black man. Peace. We're all the same. Peace. Strange how the most intelligent people say that. Peace. Because we are all hungry we all eat pork, right! Peace.

History repeats. Peace. Ask yourself when was Europe last in Unified Economic Boomtime? Peace. There's a helluva lot of goats around here. Le Pen is one big billy goat. But I've been called a nigger, been spat on and snubbed more times here in England than France. Peace. I've never been to France. Peace. Antiracismmulticulturalethnicityagenda. Peace. Too many new images in old minds cause information overloads, blips and viruses. Peace. I prefer old images in new minds; truth and honesty. Peace. Love sees no colour. Peace. I love my colour, ebony brown. Peace. Without understanding, love suffocates, overpowers, smothers – we have all been there. Peace. Love sees no colour. Peace. But I am not transparent. Peace. Speak your mind. Peace. We may learn together. Peace. Breach it. Peace. Reach it.

Brinkley Park

In the interval of each footstep
a distant drunken couple laugh.
Like a lioness chewing gravel
her feet crunched the speckled path,
thinking of every memory hugging
short cut she knew so well,
she waited as walking for the
timely chime of the 3 a.m. church bell.
As she recalled the warmth
of pillow and sheet
she slowly bent under the shadow of the willow
to rub awake her sleeping feet
and it was cold, wet,
and dauntingly dark
as she stepped through
the bowels of Brinkley Park.

The trees, dew-slimy as the beads
of sweat on the face of the killer.
The mist clung to oak and grass,
like a scene from a midnight thriller
yet this was a far cry from
any television show,
as were her treacle tears with
each life sapping blow.
Shadows ripped the grass verges
into vast empty ravines,
vast and empty enough to
swallow her muffled screams.
He acted out his illness
gas to his hallucinated spark,
the day he raped Charla Leeston
in the bowels of Brinkley Park

and another woman fell victim
to the penis wrapped in barbed wire.
another woman withdrew into the attic
seeing smoke and in fear of the fire

another woman wraps herself
into one piece of clothing more,
and another woman finds
the thirteenth bolt for her security door.

Rage

Take the sea in handfuls
and spill it onto this city's streets
and no one will notice at first
vagrants will laugh into the bottle
builders will point from the scaffolding
intellects will snort in mid-conversation
office workers will – glance through windows.

Taking the sea in handfuls is not a loud task.
I may sing while I am doing it.
I may skip while carrying.
I am allowed.

The glances and snorts irritate.
'Yeah – it's the sea, ha!'
It feels so triumphant to let it
trickle through my fingers into the cracked kerbs.